MAY THEY ALL BE ONE

MAY THEY ALL BE ONE

*Origins and Life
of the Focolare Movement*

by
Chiara Lubich

New City Press

Published in the Philippines and the United States by
New City Press, 4800 Valenzuela Street, Sta. Mesa, Manila
and New City Press, 202 Cardinal Rd., Hyde Park, NY 12538
© New City, Manila

Translated from the original Italian
Tutti siano Uno
© 1968, 1990 Città Nuova Editrice, Roma

ISBN 0-911782-46-X
6th printing, June 1995

Printed in the Philippines

This book is dedicated
to the increasing number of people interested
in the events and ideas
that contributed to the birth and growth
of the Focolare.
It is a brief account
of an extraordinary story
that had as its protagonists,
young people with a strong belief in the love
of a God who is Love.
This human-divine dialogue,
which has as its principal setting,
the Second World War,
is recounted by
its principal protagonist,
Chiara Lubich,
whom we thank
for providing us with this material,
of such great interest and relevance
for so many people.

Some Focolare Terms

The following brief definitions may prove helpful to those readers who are not familiar with the Focolare.

Focolare: An Italian word meaning "hearth" or "family fireside." It was the name given to the initial group by others who felt the "warmth" of their love. Focolare refers to the Movement as a whole, also known as the Work of Mary.

Focolare household: A small community of either men or women, whose first aim is to achieve among themselves the unity Jesus prayed for, through the practice of mutual love.

focolarina/o (Plural: focolarine/i): A member of a focolare household.

volunteer: The volunteers—short for "Volunteers of God"—are members of the Focolare who are particularly committed to bringing the Gospel spirit to bear on the relationships and structures of society at large.

gen: Gen is short for "New Generation," the youth movement born of the Focolare committed to living the Gospel message of love and unity, and to sharing it with other youth.

Mariapolis: Literally, City of Mary. This is the name given to the annual summer gathering of persons of all vocations, ages, and social classes whose sole purpose is to live the experience of reciprocal love. Permanent Mariapolises are little towns whose purpose is the same as the summer Mariapolises.

Ideal: The word Ideal is used in the Focolare, primarily to mean God, chosen as the one aim in life. Secondly, it also stands for the Focolare spirituality and the way it is lived in daily life.

CONTENTS

1

The Story of the Focolare

In a public audience in St. Peter's, on July 10, 1968, Pope Paul VI referred to the Focolare as a "flourishing tree, luxuriant and most fruitful."

Just as every tree begins with a small seed, so the Focolare had the humblest of origins.

Back in 1943, in the northern Italian city of Trent, there were just a few of us. We were young girls, practically children you might say, since the youngest was only fifteen. As everyone knows, young girls are readily drawn to give their hearts to an ideal. For example, I remember that my ideal in life was to study philosophy, whereas one of my friends dreamt of starting a family, and another of furnishing an elegant, stylish home.

But it was wartime. Bombs were falling, destroying parts of our city and claiming their victims. In the midst of the bombardments the Lord seemed to telling us something, young though we were: that our dreams would be shattered just like everything else around us. For example, I could not continue my philosophy studies in other cities because of the barricades, my friend could not fulfill her dream because her fiancé never returned; and the others, too, saw everything perish: homes, schools, works of art—all the things they held dear. The lesson the Lord was teaching us could be summed up in one sentence: All is "vanity of vanities" (Ecc. 1:2); everything passes away.

Confronted with such a spectacle, we looked around at all the ruins and asked ourselves: "Is there anything that does not pass away? Any reality that no bombs can destroy?" And as though someone had enlightened us from within, we answered: "Yes, there is such a reality: it is God. God endures forever."

So, driven by a supernatural force, we decided to make God the "Ideal" of our lives.

Even though we were so young, we could have lost our lives at any moment, because the shelters we had to use did not provide any real protection from the bombs. So we were constantly faced with the possibility of being called to appear before God. This ever-present thought increased our desire to find the fastest way to have God truly at the center of our lives.

When we went to the shelters (up to eleven times a day), we always took a copy of the Gospels with us. Once when we opened it we found the words:

"None of those who cry out, 'Lord, Lord,' will enter the kingdom of God but only the one who does the will of my Father in heaven" (Mt. 7:21) and "He who obeys the commandments he has from me is the man who loves me" (Jn. 14:21). Then we understood. If we wanted to have God for our "Ideal" we had to do his will, because loving God is not so much a matter of feelings as it is an act of the will. And so we sought to do his will as it was manifested to us by circumstances, by the duties of our state in life, by those in authority over us, and by the inspirations of the moment. We knew that only the present moment was in our possession, since the past was already gone and the future, even the very next moment, might find us already in the next life.

Never straying from God's will was a way of telling him concretely that we loved him.

In the days that followed, we asked ourselves: "Is there anything Jesus desires us to do that is especially pleasing to him, so that if we had to appear before him immediately, he would be pleased with us?"

Again the Gospel gave us the answer: "I give you a new commandment: love one another; just as I have loved you, you also must love one another" (Jn. 13:34 JB). So we began to look at one another in a new way and decided to make our small group a concrete expression of the commandment that Jesus had referred to as "his own."

We knew that Jesus had loved us to the point of dying for us; therefore, we had to be ready to die for one another. This led us to a kind of inner conversion, because we became determined to base our lives on constant mutual love, whatever direction they might take.

So in the morning, before going to Mass or receiving communion, we would ask ourselves: "Are we ready to die for one another?" For the Gospel says: "If you bring your gift to the altar and there recall that your brother has anything against you, leave your gift at the altar, go first to be reconciled with your brother, and then come and offer your gift" (Mt. 5:23-24).

Love had come before all else: before going to school, before going to work, before going to sleep at night.

Of course, the Lord did not always ask us to die for one another, which would have been the fullest measure of love. But he did ask us for smaller things. For example, if one of our friends was suffering, we all suffered with her and the burden was lightened. If another was happy, we rejoiced with her and the joy was multiplied. I remember that one of us had two coats while another had none, so naturally she gave the extra one to her. If I had a good idea that helped me love the Lord more, I shared it, and my companions did the same with me.

Love led us to put everything in common: our

material possessions and spiritual possessions.

We continually practiced loving one another as Jesus loved us.

What was the result?

First of all, we experienced within us the fruits of the Spirit that St. Paul speaks of: fullness of light, joy and peace.[1] Then, since we tried to have constant mutual love, and "Where charity and love abide," as the liturgy tells us, "there is God," God helped us to a better understanding of his revealed word. As I said before, we used to take the Gospels with us into the shelters, and it was like discovering them all over again: it seemed that God himself was explaining them to us.

Those words seemed so unique that everything else we read, even the works of spiritual writers, seemed watered down by comparison. They were *words of life*; they could be put into practice at once. For example, "Love your neighbor as yourself" (Mt. 19:18) could be done right away, because there was usually a neighbor nearby. Likewise, "As often as you did it for one of my least brothers, you did it for me" (Mt. 25:40) could immediately be translated into practice. Moreover, the words in the Gospels were meant for everyone. We discovered that the word of God was truly a light come from on high to illuminate every person in the world. His words were something that everyone, child or adult, learned or not, could live.

What these words produced in us and in those around us was a kind of revolution!

I must admit, that up till then, though I was a Christian and a practicing Catholic, I had not taken the word of God very seriously; the Gospel had not been my rule of life. But now, living the Gospel changed my relationship with God and with others. And the same happened to my friends.

The Gospel told us how to act, even towards our enemies: "Love your enemies, do good to those who hate you" (Lk. 6:27).

Naturally, when we started doing this, people around us began to ask: "Why do you love everyone? What makes you act this way?" We would answer simply: "Come with us and we'll tell you." Then we would explain how we had discovered an ideal to live for that would not perish. People understood, because the lesson of the war was there for everyone to see. Around our small group, a community started to form, of people that desired to live the same way.

In a few months, in the city of Trent, there were five hundred of us living the Gospel, which by its very nature bound us together and united us with one another.

The whole Gospel message became the object of our reflection and our new rule of life.

Certain phrases stood out for us from the very

beginning, especially those that spoke of love of God, of love of neighbor, and of unity.

One passage, I remember, made a deep impression on us: "[Father,] that all may be one" (Jn. 17:21). This immediately led us to love everyone, without distinction, and to put ourselves at God's disposal, so that this testament of Jesus might be realized.

Another passage that attracted us was the one in which Jesus said: "Where two or three are gathered in my name, there am I in their midst" (Mt. 18:20). We had discovered the joy of this fellowship in Christ, and we did not want to lose it. We wanted to have him always in our midst.

And what did Jesus do when he was spiritually present in us? He enabled us to achieve unity and to experience what he had referred to in the Gospel, when he prayed: "That all may be one as you, Father, are in me, and I in you; I pray that they may be one in us, that the world may believe that you sent me" (Jn. 17:21).

So we went ahead, driven by the grace of God. Then, one day we read in the Gospel the words Jesus addressed to those he had just chosen to be his co-workers: "He who hears you hears me" (Lk. 10:16). And we understood that the one who could tell us if we were on the right track or not was our bishop. So we went to see him and told him everything. The bishop exclaimed: "Here I see the hand of God!" And he encouraged us to go ahead.

The Focolare spread very quickly and very widely. We attribute its global expansion to two things: our close unity with ecclesiastical authority—whose importance we rediscovered, and through which we feel more intimately united to Christ whom it represents—and the unity we have tried to have among ourselves, so that Jesus among us can witness the truth to the world and win it over to himself.

We spread throughout Italy first. Today the Focolare is present in practically every Italian city.

Beginning in 1958, the Focolare spread to other European countries; and it is now present in North and South America, Africa, Asia, and Australia. I say this simply for the glory of God, because no human effort could have accomplished all this.

The principal effects that God brings about through the Focolare are "conversions," in the sense that people are converted to God. We have seen so many non-believers turn to him! They have been struck by seeing people of many different nations, races, and social backgrounds united in the name of Jesus, just as in the first Christian communities.

Sinners have reformed and atheists have turned to God. The lukewarm have become fervent. Those who thought themselves "good enough" have become apostles of the love of Christ and of neighbor.

Another effect that Christ in our midst brings

about is vocations: so many young men have entered the priesthood and now live in unity with one another and with their bishops!

So many religious orders have been renewed by this spirit! After all, what is the fundamental spirit of the Focolare? It is love, as love is understood in the New Testament, which tells us, "God is Love" (1 Jn. 4:8).

When this love enters monasteries and convents, God himself becomes more fully present and produces changes there, too. For example, the religious become more united with God and with their superiors, and the various religious orders become more united among themselves.

Another result: God is entering the secular world. The laity, filled with this spirit, become the kind of Christians the Second Vatican Council hoped for and desired. The Council said that the whole Church should be apostolic and missionary, and that includes the laity. It also said that the whole Church should strive for holiness, and that too means the laity. We know that holiness consists in love; and through love God enters families, schools, factories, government, and so on. There are countless families where father, mother, and children are united in living the Gospel and in sharing their personal experiences, so they can advance in the love of God; and they are transforming the fabric of society around them.

This spirit of love is bringing about what Pope Pius XII called the "consecration of the world."

Because of this spirit, the laity are waking up and realizing that they too are the Church; and they want to work with the hierarchy in the renewal and building up of the Church for the glory of God.

These are the main characteristics of the Focolare. One might ask: "Well, what's so new about all that?" Nothing really. What is new is the commitment to live the Gospel in this way today. What is also new, perhaps, is the greater stress that we put on certain Gospel values and truths: mutual love, Jesus in our midst, living as the Mystical Body, unity, a real sense of the Church. These are values that were always in the Gospel, but it seems God is bringing them more into relief today. Just think how much the whole Christian world today speaks of love, fellowship, and community.

Until 1960, the Focolare was made up entirely of Catholics, and did not have any real contact with Christians of other communions. We thought that the Focolare was meant by God for the Roman Catholic Church. None of us were thinking of ecumenism. But it was God who planned the development of the Focolare, not ourselves. In 1960 we met some Lutherans. We told them our story, and above all we tried to love them. They became very interested. First they put us in touch with some *Bruderschaften*, Lutheran communities of both married and celibate members, some of whom live a community life. Then some pastors asked us to speak to them and to meet their congregations. And some theologians invited us to speak to their colleagues. At the same time, these Lutherans wanted to get to know the Catholic Church, especially in Italy. We went with them to Assisi, Florence, Trent, Rome, Naples, and many other places; and there was always an atmosphere of sincere mutual love.

For them too, this way of life brought about a kind of rediscovery of the Gospel. They set about living it, and introduced this practice into their parishes and religious communities. This dialogue and sharing have continued ever since. We now know thousands of Lutherans, whom we regard as our dear brothers and sisters in Christ. They are such, not only because of our common baptism, but also because of our common effort to live the Gospel, especially in the spirit of mutual love.

Together, we want to have Jesus in our midst, since our baptism makes this possible. And of one thing we are certain: Jesus is *the* Theologian; and in our midst he is not only Love, he is also Truth. If we try to live so that he is always in our midst, and if we first seek those things which unite us, as Pope John XXIII used to say, then Jesus in our midst will gradually clarify the truth to us, and work out any theological differences which still separate us.

Everyone knows that Lutherans have difficulty with some things concerning the Catholic Church, but through our contacts, we have seen many of those difficulties fade. For example, whenever the Lutherans come to Rome, they have an audience with the Pope, and they have learned to love him. And they have also shown a desire to get to know our bishops and religious orders.

For our part, we have come to know and appreciate the great love the Lutherans have for the word of God, and their deep spirit of prayer.

Getting to know one another has helped us to love one another, and we have discovered that we are brothers and sisters. We have seen how much we have in common.

Twice I have had an audience with the Lutheran bishop of Bavaria, Dr. Dietzfelbinger, who has since been elected President of the Lutheran Church in Germany. He loves our spirituality,[2] and has always supported our ecumenical efforts.

At one point we felt the need for this contact between Catholics and Lutherans to be continuous. With the permission of our respective Church authorities and the blessing of the local Catholic bishop, Josef Stimpfle, a center has been established at Augsburg, Germany, where Catholics and Lutherans can continue to grow in knowledge, love and appreciation of one another.

In 1965, at a meeting of Catholics and Lutherans at our Mariapolis Center in Rocca di Papa near Rome, some Anglican priests were present. They were very pleased with the family-like atmosphere of the meeting. That was the start of a mutual sharing with Anglicans, which has brought immense results. How many things we did not know about the Anglican Church, but have now come to appreciate! And how many things they did not know about the Roman Catholic Church!

The Archbishop of Canterbury, Dr. Ramsey, invited me to come to London to meet him; and after I had explained something of the Focolare, he told me: "I am filled with gratitude to God for his hand in this work. You have much to offer to the Church of England. There are many ways in which you can work with Anglicans in this country and have spiritual communion with them, so that their hearts can be warmed by the fire of this spirit."

In the last few years we have had many contacts with various Christian denominations in North and South America.

Thus, the Focolare, once present only in the Catholic Church, is now striking roots among Christians of many other Churches, who all strive to live its spirit as they understand it, to whatever extent they can.

Some years ago, I was in the Holy Land, at a

time when Christians of various Churches were quarreling over their rights to the holy places. I remember the sorrow I felt at the Holy Sepulcher. Even this holy place was divided, and belonged to three different Christian denominations. Jerusalem seemed like the city of Christian disunity!

But it was there, right at the sepulcher, that I found hope. I wondered: "Why are they quarreling for a part of Jesus' sepulcher? Why? Because they love Jesus." And I thought: "The day will come when all Christians will understand that loving God means doing his will, and since his great desire is that we love one another, they will no longer quarrel among themselves. Instead, they will love one another, and the sepulcher will belong to everyone. And so will the Church."

When our Christian brothers and sisters of other Churches come to Rome, and we go together to visit the catacombs and the Colosseum, where we remember the martyrs; or we go to the Basilicas of St. Paul and St. Peter and all the other wonderful Christian sites in the Eternal City, I often feel like saying: "All this is yours; it belongs to us all, because here our ancestors were united!"

And when I go to Germany, for example, and see those magnificent Gothic churches that the Lutherans have, I feel like saying to my friends: "Why don't we put everything we have in common? We would all gain from it."

Unfortunately that has not yet happened!

I remember, however, that in 1966, some Anglicans, some Lutherans, and I visited Loppiano, an ecumenical town of ours near Florence that gives a Christian witness of mutual love; and where Jesus is present in the midst of all. There we were all struck by the same thought: "When it comes right down to it, we all share this spirituality, we are all trying to live the Gospel. The Catholic Church has approved the Focolare and our brothers and sisters of other Christian Churches can belong to it, as well. Therefore, everything that belongs to us as a movement belongs not only to the Catholics, but also to the Anglicans, to the Lutherans, and to all who live this spirituality." And I said: "So our centers are yours! Our towns are yours! Our publishing houses are yours...." And the Lutherans and Anglicans who were there, knowing that their Church authorities approved of the Focolare and wanted this spirituality to spread to their Churches, answered: "And our homes are yours too!"

From this desire a hope was born: that since what is humanly impossible is possible for God, if we, in our various denominations, have God in our midst, all things will be possible. Yes, because in our hearts we feel deeply that, as an Anglican bishop said one Easter at a meeting of the Focolare in Rome, the more we know one another, the more the division becomes intolerable.

An old proverb says, "Last is best," and so now we come to the final event in our historical sketch: our encounter with the Orthodox Church.

We had already met individual Orthodox leaders, but our real encounter with this elect portion of God's Church occurred when some of us met with Patriarch Athenagoras on June 13, 1967.

I surely don't need to tell you about the Patriarch. I will just say this: "How humble and holy a person he must be, if for him, God inspires a pope to leave Rome to go and embrace him!" And that is what happened on July 25, 1967.

The Patriarch has gotten to know the Focolare and hopes that its spirit will spread.

May God help us then, and if it be his will, may he make us all instruments in bringing about the unity of his one Church.[3]

2

The World Was Not So Dark Anymore

The Focolare began as a result of an encounter with God, who alone has given meaning to the whole of its life and development.

Like the morning sun, he radiated his presence on a world that was rediscovering peace after the long nightmare of war. And he offered to us his children a life more divine—and therefore more Christian, more unified, more harmonious—than the good lives some of us were already leading.

Young women in other places and times, and under other circumstances, had also been called to this same ideal of life. One whom we frequently recalled was St. Clare.

"What is it you want, my child?" St. Francis had asked her when she ran away from home at the age of eighteen to follow the Lord.

"God," had been her simple answer.

We too, helped by grace, had discovered that in God—the only absolute reality—we would find all we had ever longed for. And our most fervent desire was to be faithful to him for the rest of our lives, just as the saints had been.

God. God alone. Any other person or thing would have detracted from the enchantment of that divine call.

For us, from the very first instant, God was synonymous with love; he was Love itself. For Scripture told us, "God is love" (1 Jn. 4:8).

God was everything for us. And he was love.

Considering the way we were accustomed to living our spiritual lives, this was something radically new; so new, in fact, that it brought about a kind of conversion.

Previously, even though we tried to be good Christians and to live in God's grace, we were spiritually like orphans who had only an earthly father and mother. But with this new understanding that God is Love, came a new awareness that we were children of our heavenly Father. In our own way, we too found ourselves saying with St. Francis, "I no longer say: 'My father, Peter Bernardone,' but 'Our Father who art in heaven.'"[4] For us there was a new bond between heaven and earth, a new relationship was being established between Father and children.

It seemed like a new faith had matured within us.

It was not just faith in God, which we had had before, but faith in his love. Nothing seemed to express better the new life upon which we had embarked than the passage: "We have come to know and to believe in the love God has for us" (1 Jn. 4:16). Our lives, from then on, were profoundly influenced by this faith in the love God has for each and every one of us and for the entire human race.

God loved us! He was our Creator. He was sustaining us moment by moment. He was our all! Our lives on this earth would be meaningless unless we were small flames of his infinite fire: love responding to Love.

So sublime was the dignity to which he had elevated us, so exalted yet so unmerited this possibility of loving him, that we often said: "We shouldn't say: 'We *have* to love God,' but 'Oh, *to be able* to love you, Lord! To be able to love you with this little heart of ours!'"

We tried hard to do this, and as the days, weeks, and years went by, it seemed that God did not want to let himself be outdone in generosity.

Scripture says: "Anybody who loves me... I shall love... and show myself to him" (Jn. 14:21 JB). Perhaps for this reason, God began to reveal to us the treasures he had provided for us in this world: that is, the various ways he was present with us in this place of exile where we await our heavenly home. His presence demonstrated ever more clearly

how boundless was his love for us and how endless
the manifestations of his fatherly care. He showed
us where we might find him in order to become more
like him. He showed us how we could possess him.
In other words, he showed us the ways and means
by which we could establish a relationship with him,
and by which this relationship could grow and ma-
ture.

He did not want us in a hermitage, or in a mon-
astery or convent, but out where the Prince of this
world rules and darkness prevails: "[Father,] I do not
ask you to take them out of the world, but to guard
them from the evil one" (Jn. 17:15).

We discovered, like infants opening their eyes for
the first time, that God's coming upon earth out of
love for us had radically changed the world, because
he had remained with us.

As we walked about the city, or traveled to different cities and countries, it was not the beautiful and
interesting things around us that attracted us. Not
even Rome's wonderful monuments and precious
relics seemed so important.

Rather, what gave a sense of continuity to our
journeying through the world for Jesus, was his
Eucharistic presence in the tabernacles we found
wherever we went.

Thus every church that came to view through the
train window was "home" for our spirits.

And when we had the opportunity to visit some place of pilgrimage, or even when we were fortunate enough to visit the Holy Land and see the places where our Savior had lived and died—places we hated to leave—the one who gave renewed vigor to our spiritual lives was Jesus in the Eucharist, equally present in every corner of the earth, whether in a remote alpine chapel or in the majestic cathedral of a great city. His presence was a light his love had enkindled here and there as a comfort to young and old, rich and poor, learned and ignorant. He was everybody's Brother, equally accessible to all, who dried every tear, restored every heart, and gave his Spirit to everyone who lived by his commands.

The world was not so dreary after all. Jesus in the Eucharist had transformed it into a vast sanctuary and was offering himself to us to assuage the hunger for the divine that lies so deeply within our hearts.

But that was not all.

Grace prompted us to see each neighbor—classmate or beggar, sales clerk or politician, infant or invalid—in a new way: We learned to recognize that each was a member of the Mystical Body, to be loved as such. And we learned to recognize and love Christ in each person.

So it was, that those who could have been an obstacle to us in our journey toward God, became instead a help.

It was just as the Scriptures had promised: "We have passed out of death and into life, and of this we can be sure because we love our brothers" (1 Jn. 3:14 JB).

The more we loved Christ in everyone, empty of ourselves, the more our hearts were filled with God. And when we recollected ourselves in the evening to pray, it was easier for the Lord to make his gentle presence felt in our hearts.

This experience made us realize how much it pleases God when we love, and showed us that to love one another as brothers and sisters was the quintessence of the Gospel.

In some of our brothers, however, we were not only to love God but also to obey him. These were our ecclesiastical superiors, the bishops and their co-workers, given charge over us by our loving Mother, the Church. They were the shepherds and we the flock.

Our conscious efforts to live in the Church, Christ's spouse, as children of God and branches united to the vine, had this effect on ourselves and on the whole of the Focolare: as time went on, our hearts seemed to beat in unison with the Church, and we could not help but feel what she felt, sharing in her struggles and victories. And we were even eager to shed our blood for her sake, with the help of God's grace.

Then came the discovery of God in our midst.

The first days we tried to live the words of Jesus, "Where two or three are gathered in my name, there am I in their midst" (Mt. 18:20), we felt as if we were in heaven, as if paradise were in our midst. Christ, in whom we were sisters and brothers, now came among us spiritually; and as he had done in Emmaus, he enkindled in our hearts a flame that the world did not know; that made everything recede into the shadows except those things that were great and beautiful and good in God's sight.

This presence of Jesus among Christians was like a church, whose "columns" were the hearts of his united children, a church that could be erected anywhere, a spiritual tabernacle that could offer the comfort of Jesus' presence, even in a noisy street, in a non-Christian land, or in a prison amidst persecution.

Jesus is always life and fullness, joy and paradise, guide and teacher. Our mutual love was the powerful means of rendering him present. We used to say: "If we crossed some logs on top of a mountain and ignited them at night, the fire would be seen all over the valley, and shine like a fallen star. But if we unite our hearts by loving one another as he has loved us, we shall have Love—who is Fire itself—burning in our midst, and we will be able to be God's instruments for many others."

So we found God in the Eucharist, we loved him in our brothers and sisters, obeyed him in our superiors, and found him spiritually present in our midst.

And the infinite God was also present in our finite hearts, through grace. We had to help him reign there in majesty, so he could destroy our ego and transform us into himself.

God was also present in Scripture, which we studied and pondered under the action of the Spirit and the guidance of the Church. It was an inexhaustible gold mine, from which those who desire to love God have drawn and will continue to draw till the end of time; like Mary, our Blessed Mother, who meditated in its words.

We wanted to imitate Mary, who had remained in the midst of the world, as best we could; so that we too could learn to give God to those around us and to the whole world.

God
Everywhere
Always
Filling the void left by sin
Overabundantly made up for by the blood of Jesus.
God is Love
Our Ideal
Aim and goal of our life.

3

A Sunbeam for Everyone

We wanted to love God.

But how were we to love him?

Not those who say "Lord, Lord," but those who do his will are the ones who love him.[5]

Loving God, then, was not a matter of feelings but of the will: it meant doing his will.

A simple but significant occurrence during those early days gave us an opportunity to put this truth into practice immediately.

One of us had consecrated herself to God with a private vow of chastity. Some time later, however, she felt the Lord was calling her to give him *everything*.

As she thought about those things she might not yet have given to the Lord, she felt that she should offer him her will under obedience, give away her few possessions to embrace poverty, and leave her family and career behind, by withdrawing completely from the world. She decided that God was calling her to enter the cloister.

Even though she did not feel inclined to that kind of life, she uttered her "yes." However, when she took this matter to her confessor, he advised her against it and told her that she had more to offer by continuing her apostolate in the world. She obeyed him, and this taught us all that what we should be concerned about, was not whether one state of life was more perfect than another, but rather, what God's will was for *us*, for each one of us.

We were greatly impressed by the words of St. Francis de Sales: "One who loves God is so completely transformed into the will of God that he can be called by that name: 'Will of God'... that is why the Lord says in Isaiah that he will call the Christian Church by a new name which he will inscribe on the hearts of the faithful... and this name will be 'My will in her.' The most noble title Christians can have is: 'The will of God in them.'"[6]

It was very clear to us then, that even though we, like so many others in the world, had thought the way to holiness quite difficult to find, there was a way open to everyone—married and unmarried, priests and factory workers, children and senior citizens, members of religious communities and members of government.

That way was called the will of God.

This simple discovery was the source of great

happiness for us. We felt that we now possessed a key to holiness that we could offer to all those we would encounter in life's journey, including the ordinary man or woman on the street.

Our primary goal was to become *God's will for us*, and thus make our choice of God a concrete reality.

At this point, we asked ourselves, "How many years do we still have on this earth? Twenty? Thirty? Or is it perhaps only a few months or days?" We saw two roads before us: we could either spend this time following our own will, or we could follow God' will. People usually follow their own will, with the consequence that, even though they may not sin seriously, they join the vast throng of those who within fifty or a hundred years are completely forgotten.

If we tried, instead, to follow God's will, offering ourselves like a chalice to hold it, gradually it would no longer be we who lived, but Christ who would live in us.

We did not know where he would lead us, but it was not difficult to entrust ourselves to the Lord, once we had discovered that he was love. The tone of melancholy resignation with which we Christians say, "God's will be done," when faced with difficult situations, seemed strange and inappropriate. When we were doing God's will, we saw nothing to be sad or resigned about. On the contrary, it seemed to us that we had to sadly resign ourselves when choosing to do our own will, which would lead us nowhere and fill us with frustration; since we were created for the infinite fulfillment that our heavenly Father has lovingly planned for us.

The saints had done God's will. That was were their true greatness lay.

In our sincere desire to reach holiness as they had, we at first imitated them by copying their actions, like children copying every adult move. We learned from them, all those bodily and spiritual mortifications you read about in books: sleeping on the ground, staying up all night in prayer, and so on.

But we often said: "If one has to pray to become a saint, then we will pray all day long; if one has to wear a hair shirt, we will wear it night and day; if one has to scourge yourself, we'll do it. But what *should* we do? What is God asking of us?"

We came to realize that we were to imitate the saints, above all, by doing God's will as they had always done. In fact, it was their doing God's will that had made each of them a divine masterpiece, reflecting the infinite splendor of his love. Only in this way, would physical and spiritual mortifications also find their proper place in our lives.

We wanted to love God by doing his will.

But God and his will are one and the same. So to live in God's will is to live in God.

A few simple, but useful, illustrations helped clarify these for us.

God was like the sun. The individual rays of sunlight touching each of us were God's will for that particular person. There was only one sun, but there were many rays, all rays of the same sun.

There was one God and one divine will, which, though one, was different for each person.

Each of us had to stay in his or her own ray, and never wander out of it.

And we had to keep in that ray for the time that was given us: now, later, tomorrow, and so on. We had to do God's will in this very moment, and then, when that moment was past, in the next moment, up till that last moment, on which our eternity would depend. We were not to stray into the past or fantasize about the future. We had to entrust the past to God's mercy, since it was beyond our control; and the future would not be ours until it became the present.

Only the present was ours. It was in the present that we had to concentrate all our mind, heart, and strength on carrying out God's will, so that he might reign in our lives.

Just like a traveler on a train would not think of walking through the cars to get to his destination sooner, but remains seated and lets the train carry him forward; so too, if we want to reach God, we needed to do his will wholeheartedly in the present moment, because time moves forward on its own.

And we knew it would not be very hard to discover what God wanted of us, because he manifests his will through superiors, through the Scriptures, through the duties of our state in life, through circumstances, inspirations, and so on. Moment by moment, illumined and aided by actual grace, we would grow toward sanctity; or rather, since we would be doing the will of Another—of God himself—he would "build up" himself in us.

Still, in the beginning, since we were not too familiar with this new life, and obviously we could not be running every moment to our spiritual director, sometimes we were a little uncertain about what the Lord expected of us.

So when we had to decide between two equally good or indifferent actions, we would ask God's help and choose one of them. We trusted in his love, and were sure that if it were not his will, he would put us back on the right track.

And so we gradually got accustomed to listening with greater attention to that inner "voice,"[7] that helps us to understand God's will, expressed in many different ways. And we learned to distinguish that voice from the many voices of our own will and of the "old self."[8]

This is the way we lived. We were certain that, as

time went on, we would see the Lord weave a beautiful design with our lives, like a divine tapestry.

As the world views things, from a purely human standpoint, the design would seem spoiled by the knots of thread here and there, where, from time to time, we had forsaken the will of God out of human weakness, and had afterward cast ourselves on his mercy so as to get back on the right track again. But from God's point of view, from which "all things work together for the good of those who love him" (Rom. 8:28), we would be able to see the magnificent design of his love in all its splendor.

And this design would be interwoven with other designs, those of the lives of all the other people who, like us and with us, had done God's will. And the whole pattern would be the work of God, who alone is able to guide our lives, put order in them, and bring them harmoniously together.

Later on we began to glimpse a little of all this.

In the very first months, the Lord fixed in our hearts the key points of the spirituality that was to animate us and the movement which was starting to spread irresistibly around us.

Then, during the years that followed, he gradually made clear to us the features that were to characterize this movement he had raised up in his Church.

At various times in our history, the Church asked

us for a description of the Focolare.

Each time, we tried hard to distill from the Focolare's life the principles that seemed to guide it; and each time the Church encouraged us to continue following those guidelines, that we felt had come from God.

The Church intervened many times to give advice, and to ask that we rewrite the Rule, till we came up with the one we joyfully and gratefully possess today as God's will for us, given to us through the hands of the Church.

The Church's intervention in our regard was a most loving one: like a mother who sees, respects, and gives approval. Obeying her, we continue to experience our true freedom as children of God.

God's will! Allow me to say again that, by God's grace, we have believed in love, and God has not disappointed us.

Today the Focolare, now officially approved, has taken its place alongside the thousands of other movements in the Church, that through the years and—we hope—down through the centuries, will continue to advance along the path of God's will.

4

The New Commandment

When a person immigrates to a new country, especially one less developed than his own, he brings with him his own customs and way of doing things. Of course he adapts, where necessary, to his new environment, but he often continues to speak his native language, dress in his accustomed fashion, and build in the style of his homeland.

When the Word of God took on our human nature, he adapted himself to our ways. He was first an infant, then a model son, and as an adult, he worked for a living. But he brought his own lifestyle with him from heaven, and sought to establish it as a new world order based on the law of heaven, which is love.

These are the thoughts that came to us while we were still suffering the scourge of war.

Perhaps that was why, when we lovingly opened

the Gospels or other books of the New Testament, during those long hours in the shelters, the passages that caught our attention were ones that spoke explicitly of love: "Only one thing is required" (Lk. 10:42), "Love your neighbor as yourself " (Mt. 19:18), "Love your enemies" (Mt. 5:44), "Love one another" (Jn. 15:17), "Above all, let your love for one another be constant" (1 Pt. 4:8).

These words seemed revolutionary to us, the key to a fullness of life we had not known before. We felt they had the power to radically transform people's lives, even the lives of us present-day Christians, as no other words could.

Even though we realized that love was the basic principle of the Gospel, the "bond of perfection," we did not immediately understand how to put it into practice, with whom to live it, or to what extent we should apply it.

At first, as we responded to the distressing circumstances of the war, we directed our efforts to the poor, in whose emaciated and sometimes repulsive faces we were sure we would find the face of the Lord.

It was a real education for us. We were not accustomed to loving, in the supernatural sense of the word. At most, we extended our esteem and friendship to our relatives and friends, but this hardly distinguished us from those who did not share our faith.

But now, impelled by God's grace and entrusting ourselves to his providence, which looks after the birds of the air and the flowers of the field, we directed our attention to all the poor of the city. We invited them into our homes and sat them at our table. It was a great honor for us to have them seated at the head of the table, to offer them the finest tableware, the best food. When we were unable to invite them into our homes, we would meet them at appointed places and give them whatever we collected. We would visit them in their wretched hovels and try to obtain medicine for them.

The poor were truly the object of our love, because in them we were able to love Jesus. They also became the concern of many other persons who were attracted by our ideal of life. As the community around the original group of us continued to grow, opportunities increased for aiding and helping those who were suffering or in want. It was quite a sight to see, and it seemed more the handiwork of angels than of human beings. Those huge piles of provisions, clothing, and medicine were an accustomed abundance in the last years of the war, and a clear sign to everyone of the special intervention of Divine Providence.

Our lives were frequently brightened, and our spiritual resolve strengthened, by small but significant happenings, which had something supernatural about them, and thus seemed to us a confirmation that the Lord was with us.

"Lord, we need a pair of shoes for you, size ten," we would pray before the Blessed Sacrament, meaning: "for you in that poor and needy person."

"Lord, we need a man's jacket for you...."

And not infrequently, it would happen that, on leaving church, we would meet a friend who would offer a pair of shoes the right size, or a man's jacket, or whatever we had prayed for.

Little things like this happen to every follower of Jesus who understands the words, "Ask and you will receive" (Mt. 7:7), but they never ceased to fill us with wonder. We were also encouraged by the extraordinary feats of those great men and women who had gone before us, and who also experienced—before they became saints—the difficulties of the ascent to God, as their hardened human personalities were thawed in the fire of divine love.

Hadn't St. Catherine loved the poor so much, that she gave one of them her cloak, and another the cross from her rosary? And didn't Jesus appear to her the next night, to thank her for the gifts she had given him in the poor?

Hadn't St. Francis given his cloak to the poor on some thirty different occasions?

So it was no great sacrifice for us to take off our winter gloves and give them to someone who had to spend hours out in the snow begging.

Moreover, we found that loving our neighbor

awakened in us a desire for greater social justice.

We had; the poor had not.

The rich had; the destitute had not.

Why not voluntarily give up whatever we could do without—everything that was superfluous—and give it to those who were dying of hunger and cold, so as to raise their standard of living through the countless little acts of relief that Christian love might suggest?

We tried to do this.

In a short time, the Focolare numbered several hundred people; and since about thirty of these were suffering from hunger, the others undertook to offer them month by month whatever they could spare, until work or some other arrangement could be found for them. We felt we could truly say of our community what had been said of the early Christians: "None of their members was ever in want" (Acts 4:34 JB).

This work went on vigorously for months.

Yet, despite the outstanding generosity of many individuals, we sensed that something more was needed if society was to be delivered of its misery; and we began to realize that perhaps this was not the immediate goal God had in mind when he prompted us to show our love in concrete ways.

Later we began to understand that he had led us to that direction for a very specific reason: it is in love, and through loving, that we come to a better understanding of the things of heaven, and that God can more easily enlighten our hearts.

It was probably this exercise in loving that taught us to open our hearts, not only to the poor, but to all people without distinction.

There certainly were people who needed food, drink, and clothing; but many also needed instruction, counsel, support, and prayer.

Opportunities for corporal and spiritual works of mercy lay before us in every direction. These, after all, would be the subject matter of the questions our Judge would ask us on the Last Day, when our eternal future would be decided. We were filled with a sense of adoration at the thought of Jesus' infinite love in revealing this to us when he came on earth, so as to facilitate our getting into heaven.

Such love inspired us all to respond with love, by doing these things which were his will.

God asked us to love not only the destitute, but each neighbor—whoever he or she might be—as we loved ourselves.

So if someone was weeping, we tried to weep with that person and the cross was lightened. If someone was rejoicing, we rejoiced with him or her and the joy was increased: "Rejoice with those who rejoice, weep with those who weep" (Rom. 12:15).

This was Christian life. This was Life. Because, it was in this constant practice of love toward each person who passed our way—rich or poor, learned or simple, man or woman, adult or child, white or black—that we understood, as never before, the truth of St. John's words: "We have passed out of death and into life, and this we can be sure because we love our brothers" (1 Jn. 3:14 JB).

Of course we ran into difficulties, because of the imperfections we all revealed in our daily dealings with one another. But we decided not to look upon each other in a merely human fashion—seeing the speck in the other's eye while forgetting the beam in our own—but rather, with a readiness to forgive and forget. We felt such a strong need to practice this mutual forgiveness, in imitation of God's mercy to us, that we made a kind of pact of mercy: we would get up every morning and see one another as completely *new* persons, who had never displayed any of those imperfections.

But one part of the Gospel message, that seemed especially beautiful and new to us, was the love Jesus wanted us to have for our enemies, be they near or far away.

This meant offering the other cheek and going the second mile, as the Gospel taught: "When a person strikes you on the right cheek, turn and offer him the other... Should anyone press you service for one mile, go with him two miles" (Mt. 5:39,41).

And so we tried to do that, whenever we met a hostile person along our way.

Lastly, the heart of the Good News: mutual love. "I give you a new commandment: love one another; just as I have loved you, you also must love one another" (Jn. 13:34-35 JB).

How had Jesus loved us? What was the measure of his love for us? Death on a cross. So we had to be ready to die for one another: "There is no greater love than this: to lay down one's life for one's friends" (Jn. 15:13).

We had to be ready, then, to perform any act of love for one another, no matter how great or how small, since giving our life was to be the measure of our love.

This meant being always ready to give whatever material possessions we had. One day, in the first focolare house, we took our few modest belongings out of the wardrobe and piled them in the center of the room. Then we gave each one what little she needed and gave the rest to the poor. We were ready to put in common our salaries as well; and all our possessions, great and small—whatever we had or whatever we would have in the future.

We were also ready to share our spiritual possessions.

Even the desire for personal sanctity had taken second place to our central commitment to God alone, that excluded every other lesser goal (but, of course, included the sanctity God had in mind for each of us).

And so, in a spirit of mutual love, we shared the beautiful experiences that this new life brought us, which were the fruit of the love that now illumined our lives. This was the only debt we wanted to have: "Owe no debt to anyone except the debt that binds us to love one another" (Rom. 13:8). Besides, when Jesus came on earth he said: "I have made known to you all that I heard from my Father" (Jn. 15:15).

So, as occasion provided, and within the limits dictated by prudence, we shared our spiritual "goods" for our mutual upbuilding; and this became a characteristic feature of our lives, particularly those of us called to live in community. And this helped us to experience the reality expressed in the words of Scripture: "Our homeland is in heaven" (Phil. 3:20 JB). Our days, which before were filled with boredom and so much of the human dimension, were now filled with talk of "heavenly" things, thus satisfying our hearts' deep desire to find a way to live our whole lives for God, and in God, without wasting a moment. Since "Where charity and love abide, there is God," he gradually made clear to us which thoughts, desires, and fruits came from the "old self" in us, and which proceeded from our "new self."

The words of Scripture took on a new meaning for us: "[You have learned that] you must put on the new man created in God's image, whose justice and holiness are born of truth" (Eph. 4:24).

God is love. But he is also light; and Jesus has

"come to the world as its light" (Jn. 12:46).

So the more one loves, the more one *sees*.

In 1943 the Focolare began; in 1949 it took a significant leap forward.

Although we hadn't planned it, providential circumstances made it possible for our initial group to withdraw from our regular routine that summer, and go up to the mountains for a period of rest and relaxation.

We needed to get away from the world for a while, but we could not lay aside the way of life that had become our reason for living. A small, rustic mountain cabin afforded us simple shelter.

We were alone, left to ourselves with our great "Ideal" that we tried to live moment by moment, and with Jesus in the Eucharist, the bond of unity, whom we received daily. We were alone to rest, pray, and meditate.

Thus began for us a time of special grace.

We had the impression that the Lord was opening our eyes and hearts to the kingdom of God in our midst, to the Trinity dwelling in this small cell of the Mystical Body. And it seemed to us that the Focolare was to be nothing other than a mystical presence of Mary in the Church.

Naturally, we would never have come down from that mountain—our little Mount Tabor—if God's will had not required it of us. The only thing that gave us the courage to do so, was love for Jesus crucified and forsaken in the hearts of countless people still dwelling in darkness.

In 1950 and 1951, we returned to the mountains. Immersed as we were in "things of heaven" (cf. Col. 3:1), we hardly noticed that the number of us gathering in the valley was increasing year by year. No longer were we just young women; now there were mothers, fathers, young men, and children. In the following years we had to rent lodgings in four nearby villages to accommodate all who came.

In 1951 we called our gathering a "city." This city lived by a single law: love. And love was the only requirement for admission.

There was no room for onlookers. All had to take an active part in building this joy-filled spiritual city, where everyone competed in serving the others, and willingly endured all manner of discomfort and inconvenience to be part of it.

In 1952 and 1953, priests and religious began to participate in great numbers. The religious came from a great variety of congregations; yet their different spiritualities harmonized beautifully and, at the same time, shone more splendidly as they celebrated their common brotherhood and sisterhood in Christ.

By 1954, those in the Focolare already felt that it was somehow a "Work of Mary"; and the leaders, aware of the responsibility which God had quite possibly entrusted to them, consecrated themselves to her Immaculate Heart, that they might be of service in accomplishing her purposes.

At the end of each summer, as we were united in constant mutual love and in the service of others, we felt that the Lord was guiding the Focolare's leadership to new insights about the Focolare, which then became the focal points of its life during the year that followed.

In 1955 the "city" was called "Mariapolis" (City of Mary).

In 1956 there were representatives from five continents. After the Mariapolis we felt a need to keep in touch, so as to help one another to live this life wherever we might be.

Thus, *Città Nuova* (New City) came into being, as an expression of mutual love. This love soon led to editions in all the principal languages of the world.

In 1957 the Mariapolis was host to many bishops, for whom it was an experience of the Church truly alive.

In 1958, taking our inspiration from an international exposition of the latest developments in science and technology, we decided to make the Mariapolis a little "Expo of God," which would highlight spiritual values.

By 1959, the Mariapolis was like a flower in full bloom. It was a blueprint of the City of Mary that the Focolare was called to help build in the midst of the world. The people gathered there were from twenty-seven different nations, speaking nine differ-

ent languages. In a spirit of unity, they each consecrated their own country to God, so that all peoples
together might form the one *People of God.*

Later on, we saw people deeply impressed, and
even moved to conversion, by hearing a simple account of this 1959 Mariapolis, or by seeing a filmed
documentary on it.

We often wondered why it had such repercussions.
Why was this Mariapolis so captivating? Why had it
echoed across the mountains and seas and reached
literally to the ends of the earth? We concluded: just
as Mary was a shining light, not so much in and of
herself, but because of God present in her heart, so
too, the influence that the Mariapolis was having
around the world—the fact that many were encountering Christ—was the effect, not so much of the
coming together of people of different races, ages
and social backgrounds, as of God living in the midst
of this Christian community, because of the practice
of constant mutual love.

The Mariapolis restored faith to many people and
set countless hearts beating again. The Lord alone
knows the number of those who, in the sacrament
of his mercy, experienced spiritual rebirth. All this
was because of the witness to God given by people
who came together from all over the world, as brothers and sisters, and offered their hearts to him, so
that his kingdom might become visible among them.

At the end of the summer, after all had gone home,

the echo could be heard returning from big cities and rural hamlets: "I have met the Lord!" "I have found God!" "My whole life has changed!"

Many have wept when they left the Mariapolis. Going back into the world they felt like orphans, called to believe and to trust like little children that God would let them see that dream once more, and that his almighty hand would make that dream a reality all over the world.

The Mariapolis drew people from all walks of life: married and single people of every sort, laity and priests, rich and poor. It also sent them forth into all walks of life, because it awakened in their hearts vocations of every kind.

The Mariapolis was like the city set on the mountaintop for all to see.

People would come to understand, and exclaim: "This is what the whole world should be like!"

What St. Augustine once said of the Church seemed to apply to this splendid flowering of Jesus' new commandment.

What Babel scattered
The Church gathers.
One language became many;
No wonder,
That is the work of pride.
Many languages become one;

No wonder,
That is the fruit of love.[10]

Now, some ten years since the last single Mari-apolis in the Dolomites, we can see this temporary city growing and multiplying each year: from Chile to Korea, from Australia to Paraguay, from the United States to the Philippines. More than thirty Mariapo-lises each year offer the world their beautiful and enchanting otherworldly atmosphere. And in Italy, a permanent Mariapolis has been established on the same pattern, as a lasting monument to the new commandment of Jesus. And this latest offspring of the Focolare—we can already foresee—will not be the only permanent Mariapolis.[11]

5

The Key to Unity

Christianity is a mystery of love and suffering. Thus these two themes are also the truly vital elements of the Focolare.

And just as in Christianity, love overcomes suffering, and life is victorious over death, so it is in the Focolare.

When we were just getting started in this new way of life, we used to wonder what the most beautiful thing in the world might be: was it the stars, the flowers, children, human genius, the sunset? We concluded that the most beautiful thing had to be love, the love that God has placed in the human heart; such as maternal love, and the love between brothers and sisters or close friends.

Jesus himself had raised "brotherly" love to a supernatural plane by making Christianity a community of sisters and brothers. Maternal love seemed even more beautiful to us, because it was purified by suffering, and was hence more enduring and more sacred to the human heart. Married love seemed to excel over all the others, because it was strong enough to enable two persons to set aside all other human affections to form a new family.

Love was certainly a beautiful thing. "But," we wondered, "what must God be like if he has created it? Can we, who have left everything for his sake, experience in this life something of that Love which God is?" We frequently read the writings of the saints, and got to know them one by one. We found them to be real experts on the love of God. They were authentic Christians, and because of that, they had been able to experience Love while still in this life.

St. Clare of Assisi, after praying at great length before the crucifix in the Church of San Damiano, had rejoined her companions and spoken of heavenly things that she had somehow received from the divine Lord dying on the cross.

St. Bonaventure, in his *Stimulating Power of Divine Love*,[12] taught us, that to reach the furnace of divine love, which is the heart of Christ, we had to enter through his wounds.

St. Catherine of Siena had built her spirituality around two concepts: blood and fire. She felt practically identified with that divine Fire: "I am the fire, you are the sparks."[13] She used strong words to express the necessity of passing through suffering, in order to be able to "burn." We read in her letters: "Clothe yourselves with his blood; bathe in his blood; plunge into his blood; drown yourselves in his blood; inebriate yourselves in his blood!"[14]

Each saint was like a star, different from all the others, with his or her own strong personality. Yet every one of them had found God, who is Love, by following the solemn way of Jesus' passion.

One day we heard a priest speaking about the sufferings of Christ. He said that the moment in which Jesus suffered most, was probably on Calvary, when he cried out: "My God, my God, why have you forsaken me?" (Mt. 27:46).

We discussed this, and in our desire to make good use of the one lifetime that we had, we decided to choose as our model "Jesus Forsaken"—as we referred to him in that moment of his suffering.

From that time on, we saw his face and heard his mysterious outcry in every moment of suffering in our lives.

Like everyone else, we too experienced bitter spiritual moments: darkness, aridity, the feeling of failure, loneliness, the burden of our own humanness and personal sinfulness.

But had not Jesus, at the ninth hour, experienced a darkness so overwhelming that it infinitely exceeded any darkness that we might experience?

And had not this aridity been so profound that it seemed in some mysterious way to deprive him of the consoling presence of the Father? Victor though he was, he had never appeared such a failure as at that moment. It was then that, as Son of God, he reunited us with the Father, paying the price with his own utter loneliness. Though innocent, he carried all our sins upon his shoulders, and drew down upon himself, like a divine lightning rod, the full force of God's justice.

Before, we used to let such moments drag on, hoping that somehow something would happen to change the situation. But now that we saw our little sufferings as a small sharing in his own, we would try to recollect ourselves for a moment in the depths of our hearts, and then offer these sufferings to Jesus, happy to add our tiny drop to his sea of pain. And we would go right on living, embracing his will moment by moment, loving each neighbor who came our way.

The darkness, the sense of failure, the dryness would disappear. We began to understand how dynamically divine the Christian life is, in that it only recognizes boredom, the cross, and suffering as transitory things, and it gives us a taste of life in its fullness, which is to say: the experience of resurrection, light, and hope, even in the midst of tribulation.

Later on, however, we learned that, in some instances, spiritual aridity can affect one deeply and bring on dark nights of the soul, like real purgatories that lasts for months and even years. At such times the soul no longer sees its Spouse before it, so to speak. He is trying to purify it and prepare it for his purposes; and so, by a special privilege of his love, the soul is so united with the sufferings of Christ that, as somcone has said so well, it does not even have the strength to offer, but only to suffer.

However, we were not yet aware of all this then, since we were just starting out on this way of life.

So for all of us, Jesus Forsaken was the key that continually reopened the door to union with God.

Love for Jesus Forsaken was also the means for repairing the little rifts that occurred in the unity we were experiencing as a result of our efforts to live in "constant mutual love" (cf. 1 Pt. 4:8). "Where charity and love are, there is God." His comforting presence gave meaning to the new life we had begun. Even the smallest actions we undertook out of love for him became sources of light which gave meaning to the present and made the future seem bright. And each time we experienced unity we experienced a fullness of joy. However, where there is no charity and love, God is not present. Thus at times this presence, this light, this joy would vanish, because of the pride or conceit of one of us, or because of someone's attachment to her own ideas or possessions, or because of a lack of love.

Then we would be confused, spiritually groping in the dark, and our past progress would seem futile. It was as though the radiant sun of unity had set.

In these moments, only the memory of Jesus, abandoned in deepest spiritual darkness, gave us hope that all was not lost, that ours was a suffering that could be pleasing to God if offered to him with love. And so we would try to do this. Then we would set about courageously trying to restore the unity among ourselves by asking forgiveness, taking the initiative even when we thought the other person was at fault. For the Gospel warned us that not even our offering at the altar was pleasing to God when mutual love was lacking.

Then the sunshine would return to our little community, the sunshine of Jesus' presence among those who are united in his name.

Love for Jesus Forsaken brought abundant light and peace, not only to our hearts, but also to the hearts of all those who, in some way, reminded us of him whom we had chosen: the lonely, the orphan, the disillusioned, the dejected, the desperate, and those who felt they were total failures or in hopeless situations. These persons were the ones especially sought out by the members of the Focolare. We would try to share some of the pain that filled their hearts. And when the moment was right, we would speak to them about Jesus, about his infinite love, about the special regard he has for the kinds of people mentioned in the beatitudes; and about the privilege it was for them to be able to help him carry his cross, for their own sake and for the sake of all humanity. We would also speak of the need to offer him our own personal sufferings, in which we were to see only his countenance.

Had not St. Thérèse of Lisieux declared: "Here is my Beloved,"[15] when she discovered her fatal illness?

Thus we and our friends gradually learned that suffering is always something sacred. We were not merely to put up with it, but to embrace it.

And so the lonely found their lives filled with God and with the companionship of the many other brothers and sisters who were already part of the Focolare. In Christ forsaken, people found direction for their lives. Orphans, in contact with these people who were trying to do God's will, found among them not only brothers and sisters, but mothers and fathers as well. The disillusioned, the weary, and the defeated resolved all their problems, because everyone's questioning found an answer in his anguished

"Why?"

In becoming a human being, Jesus had come right down to our level; but on the cross he had humbled himself to the extreme. In his abandonment he seemed reduced to nothing. Like a divine ramp between earth and heaven, he had made it possible for anyone in the world, whatever his or her moral or spiritual condition, to draw near to his divine majesty. All that was required was that one turn to Jesus and transform one's oppressive burden of sorrow into the currency of love, as he had done.

In this way, through the Focolare, many people have come to understand and experience the truth of Jesus' words: "People who are in good health do not need a doctor; sick people do" (Mt. 9:12).

And in the first Focolare household, so as to be true Christians, we would say each day on awakening: "Because you are forsaken..." as if to say: "You, my crucified Lord, under whatever guise you may come, are the reason for my life. I will not shun the encounter with you. Rather, it will be the best moment of my day."

Then there were the non-believers, the sinners, those far from God, who were like desecrated tabernacles, but were still members of the Mystical Body, or at least meant to be.

In these brothers and sisters, too, we saw his image. And our love for Jesus Forsaken in them, along with the witness of our unity, brought about all kinds of conversions, by God's grace.

There are some movements and orders in the Church whose fruits are not apparent, because the supernatural effects they produce are destined in a mysterious way for other parts of the Mystical Body, wherever God sees the greatest need. There are other religious institutes which dedicate themselves to the works of mercy and erect schools, orphanages, hospitals, and so on.

The work of the Focolare, in God's plan of grace, is the conversion of the people we meet and the leading back to God of the society in which we are immersed.

Love for Jesus Forsaken was also the means of spreading our "Ideal" throughout the world.

Without exception, the grain of wheat cast to the ground must die and decay in order to bear fruit. This was also true in our case, wherever the Focolare spread.

We underwent all sorts of trials—greater and lesser "agonies" that were not easy to get used to.

But Jesus crucified, burdened with the weight of our sins, seemed to us the divine grain of wheat, withering and dying to give us life as children of God. It was in his name and for love of him that we accepted these trials, so as to further the conversion of the world to God.

Later, when the little tree of the Focolare took root here and there in new regions and countries, we ran into additional trials that were like the pruning of which the Gospel speaks. These cut back the Focolare and caused much suffering, but when accepted with love, turned out to be for the greater good.

And for that matter, was not Jesus in his abandonment the greatest example of one who had been "pruned"? He was cut off from heaven, to give us who were separated from God the possibility of being regrafted into God.

Looking beyond the confines of the infant movement, we also tried to see and love Jesus Forsaken in the great sufferings of the Church.

We were able to see him in a special way in those portions of the Mystical Body which had been weakened by the onslaughts of secularism, materialism, and atheism, and were often suffering ill treatment, and even martyrdom, under subtle atrocious forms of persecution.

The Church in those situations seemed to reecho Jesus' cry: "My God, my God, why have you forsaken me?" and thus held a special attraction for us. It awakened in us a vocation: to bring God wherever people were without him.

Another place where we heard Jesus' cry echoing in the Church was in the division among Christians. Many of our fellow Christians were already involved in an ecumenical movement which aspired to unity.

And it seemed to us that the Lord wanted to use the Focolare on a very broad scale in the Church, to break down age-old prejudices, and to promote mutual understanding and esteem as a foundation for the unity to come.

There were also portions of the Mystical Body that were dying of spiritual anemia, in places such as Latin America, where the population was overwhelmingly Christian but where there were very few priests and bishops. These people were our brothers and sisters, heirs of the same faith; but they were living under conditions that made it practically impossible to maintain that faith. They too reminded us of Jesus Forsaken.

The whole world, from mission lands to those areas where Christ was still totally unknown, was longing for one thing: the Gospel, which alone enables people to find their true selves, because it reveals to them the Creator, in whom everything has meaning and value.

In every person, there was a silent cry of abandonment to which we were meant to respond. But to do so, we had to have the mind of Christ. We had to be *other Christs*, allowing him to live in us today, in the twentieth century, with all its special needs and problems.

Putting its faith in God, the Focolare wanted to help satisfy humanity's spiritual hunger. And we felt there was no better way of doing this than to relive, step by step, all that Jesus had said when he himself became a man for the sake of humanity; to believe and live all he taught, and make our own the prayer that was his last testament, in which he expressed his life's purpose: "Father... that all may be one" (Jn. 17:11,21).

For these reason the Focolare households have always tried to keep in touch with the many people all over the world who know this spirituality and live it. With God's grace we would like to have for each of them the love that Jesus had for his disciples—"Having loved his own who were in the world, he loved them to the end" (Jn. 13:1 RSV)—so that all of us throughout the world may form, in Christ who has called us, an ever-more-closely-knit "network." In this way, everyone's confidence and courage will be strengthened. Each one will feel the support of all in overcoming the trials of life, and will be better able to be a living witness of the Gospel and the Church to as many people as possible (since Jesus prayed for everyone, without exception).

This is our "Ideal": Jesus crucified and forsaken, whom we find within us and around us everywhere in the world, and whom we want to comfort and console.

Our limited experience has taught us that one cannot live the Christian life without consecrating oneself to the cross, because our experience is just one more instance of the truth of Jesus' words: "If anyone wants to be a follower of mine, let him renounce himself, take up his cross and follow me" (Mt. 16:24 JB).

But as a comfort to those who are embarking upon this divine adventure, we must say, that like our great brothers and sisters, the saints, we too, in our small measure, have experienced that in embracing the cross one does not find only suffering. On the contrary, one finds love, the Love that is the life of God himself within us.

6

The Word of Life

A practice that characterized the Focolare from the very beginning is what we call the *Word of Life*.

Before we took up this new life, one of us, who was sincerely and ardently searching for truth, had thought that to do so she had to study the secularistic philosophies being taught at the universities. And she had done this, while continuing in good faith to be a devout and practicing Christian.

But then, as the war raged on, we made a new "discovery."

It was simple, but profound in its implications: Jesus was the Truth, and if we wished to find the Truth we had to follow him, the Word Incarnate.

His truth was to be found in the Gospel, verse by verse, word by word.

Huddled in a small circle in the damp stone shelters, we would lovingly read God's word by the light of a candle. The words leapt out and illuminated our hearts with an unaccustomed brilliance. Never had the Gospel seemed so unique and engrossing; never had it seemed so new to us.

Written with divine precision, it offered us real *words of life*, that we could put into practice. By comparison, the greatest spiritual writings seemed watered down, and the words that filled our books of learning and philosophy simply paled to nothingness. The word of God was rich with meaning and inspiration; it could be applied to every situation.

The word of God—each word of God—was something that could be lived by every person on earth: ourselves, our friends, the people who lived two centuries ago, and those who will live in the twenty-first century—blacks, whites, homemakers, congressmen, farmers, convicts, children, grandparents.

We read: "Unless your righteousness exceeds that of the scribes and Pharisees, you will never enter the kingdom of heaven" (Mt. 5:20 RSV); "[Forgive] seventy times seven" (Mt. 18:22); "Give to the man who begs from you" (Mt. 5:42).

Jesus was "the real light which gives light to every man" (Jn. 1:9). God's becoming a human being was not an everyday event; and the chance to hear words of eternal life was not something to take lightly. So we felt it was wise and expedient, in this short life of ours, to listen to the divine words Jesus had spoken to us human beings, and put them into practice.

So strong was this conviction God had put into
our hearts, and so urgent the need to act on it, that
we often encouraged one another to live in such a
way that even if the impossible were to happen, and
all the New Testaments in the world were to be
destroyed, people could practically rewrite the Gospels by looking at the way we lived: "Blest are you
who are weeping" (Lk. 6:21); "Blest are they who
show mercy" (Mt. 5:7); "Stop passing judgment"
(Mt. 7:1); "Love your enemies" (Mt. 5:44).

Every week we concentrated on living according
to some particular "word."

We carried it in our hearts like a treasure and tried
to apply it every chance we had.

But we did not stop there. Since we were trying
to live in constant mutual love, we wanted to share
our spiritual wealth with one another, so as to con-
tribute to one another's growth in holiness as though
it were our own. We shared how we tried to live
according to the Word of Life, and the results; as
well as our wonderment and joy at seeing that it
was changing our lives. We began to realize how
worldly our lives had been previously. We had been
Christians, but our mentality had still been far from
that of Jesus.

"In so far as you did this to one of the least of
these brothers of mine, you did it to me" (Mt. 25:40

JB). We realized that Jesus wanted to be loved in our brothers and sisters, even in the lowliest. Consequently, the various human considerations about others being pleasant or unpleasant, attractive or ugly, dull or agreeable, young or old, all gave way to this single thought: it was Jesus we were to love in our brother or sister. It was him we were to see; and we had to treat each person as we would want Jesus to be treated.

The words, "Whoever listens to you, listens to me" (Lk. 10:16) deepened our faith in the teaching authority of the Church. We knew how easy it was, even with good intentions, to go astray, especially when interpreting Scripture. So we would submit our little commentary on the weekly Word of Life to our archbishop for approval. He would amend and endorse it.

You could say it was our "interpretation"; but in the same sense that an actor, for example, interprets a script written by someone else, under the guidance of a director. Our task was to *live* the Gospel, written by St. Luke, St. Matthew, etc., and to live it today, under the guidance of the Church; so as to gradually become other present-day Christs, in whatever location God had chosen to place us.

We were to do this, not merely by remaining in the state of grace—which could simply mean avoiding sin—but by a progressive "reevangelization" of our lives.

A person could live to be ninety and still be illiterate, if he or she did not know the alphabet and a few rules of grammar. In the same way, a Christian would not know how to live like Jesus, if he or she did not listen to the words of God and put them into practice. One had to learn to live them one by one.

In living this way for years, we discovered countless treasures in the Gospel.

We gained a more profound and accurate understanding of love, as we practiced prudence, simplicity, purity, poverty, compassion, and so on. And at the same time, all these virtues acquired a deeper, truer meaning, as ways of expressing our love for God and neighbor.

This experience was so vivid, that after being nourished for a long time on the word of God, we felt that every word uttered by Christ was *love*. It seemed almost as if every one of his words was equally important, and that each was as important as his testament. Just as Jesus in the Eucharist was wholly present in the host, and also in every little particle of the host, so he was present in the whole Gospel and in each "word" of the Gospel.

This experience also helped us understand the Church in a new way.

Jesus was the incarnate Word of God.

The Church seemed like the incarnation of the Gospel, and for this reason she was the Spouse of Christ.

We looked at the many religious orders that had flourished down through the centuries. Each order or religious family could be seen as an "incarnation" of some aspect of Jesus' life: an attitude of his, an event in his life, an aspect of his suffering, something he said, and so on.

For example, the Franciscans were continually proclaiming to the world by their very lifestyle: "How blest are the poor in spirit: the reign of God is theirs" (Mt. 5:3).

The Dominicans contemplated the Logos, the Divine Word, so they could explain and spread the truth.

The Jesuits emphasized obedience.

St. Thérèse and the followers of her "Little Way" seemed to immortalize the words: "Unless you change and become like little children, you will not enter the kingdom of God" (Mt. 18:3).

The Sisters of Bethlehem, of Nazareth, of Bethany, and so on, were concrete expressions of moments in the life of Jesus. The Stigmatines were a living reminder of his wounds. St. Catherine recalled his blood; and St. Margaret Mary Alacoque, his Sacred Heart.

The monks combined action and contemplation.

The Carmelites worshipped God on Mt. Tabor,

ever ready to descend and preach, and to face passion and death.

The missionaries were living out the command: "Go into the whole world and proclaim the good news to all creation" (Mk. 16:15).

The orders, congregations, and institutes for works of charity were following the example of the Good Samaritan.

Just as water crystallizes into tiny stars that make up the white snow, so also love, which has its most perfect and beautiful form in Jesus, finds various expressions in the Church, in the different orders and religious families. All the virtues had flourished, and were continuing to do so, in the splendid garden which was the Church.

Each founder of a religious order seemed to us like the personification of a particular virtue. Each of them, after being transformed by much love and suffering, had entered heaven as a "word of God."

They had accomplished the plan of God for them. And we could say of them: "The heavens and the earth will pass away but my words will not pass" (Mk. 13:31), because the saints were, and continue to be, "words of God" spoken to the world. And being so identified with God's word, they would not pass away either.

Thus the Church appeared as a majestic Christ extending through time and space, because the spiritual children of all these saints, by virtue of the catholic blood that flowed through their veins, had spread to every place on earth where God's Church was present.

From the beginning, men and women of practically all the religious orders have been part of the Focolare, because they have felt that they too could benefit from its spirituality.

In the Focolare's emphasis on evangelical love, the cross, unity, the word of God, Mary, the Church, and the Mystical Body, these religious have found a revitalization of the values that—to a greater or lesser degree—inspired their own founders.

Encountering the Focolare, and practicing its spirituality—in addition to giving them a greater zeal for the glory of God—has often led them to a rediscovery of their own Rule, and to a greater love and appreciation for their founder.

This better appreciation of their spiritual father or mother, has naturally led to a stronger bond with their spiritual brothers and sisters. The spirit of the Focolare, when well presented and properly understood, has also led to more sincere and loving obedience toward superiors. The fruit of all this was soon obvious.

For example, some orders went through a real renewal as a result of more closely observing their Rules, often with a return to their original spirit. Many orders experienced an increase of vocations, growth in their missions, new vitality in their seminaries. And those who lived this spirituality were entrusted with difficult tasks and positions of responsibility.

In the 1959 Mariapolis, the men religious alone came from more than sixty orders and congregations. All were united by a common purpose: to live as members of the Mystical Body.

It seemed that Mary, spiritually present in her city, had brought together beneath her mantle the great variety of religious habits that outwardly expressed the particular ideal of life that each order followed.

Mary, who is everyone's Mother, seemed to have decided that through the Focolare, she would put herself at the service of her son Jesus, in the many different religious orders blossoming in the Church; so that all these religious might have a greater sense of belonging not only to their particular orders, but to the one, universal Church.

When Jesus had said, "Where two or three are gathered in my name, there am I in their midst" (Mt. 18:20), he had certainly meant this to include where a Benedictine and a Franciscan, or a Carmelite and a Passionist, or a Jesuit and a Dominican were united in his name. And if he were in their midst, their encounter would make the Benedictine a better Benedictine, the Franciscan a better Franciscan, and so on. Thus the Focolare has helped the Church, in her rich diversity and profound unity, to be a more beautiful and worthy Spouse of Christ.

7

Where Two or Three

The way that the Lord had pointed out to us from the very beginning was the *way of love*—evangelical love, the love that St. Paul says believes all things, hopes all things, endures all things, is always patient, and never resentful.

We began to understand that we were to reach sanctity by loving others as we loved ourselves, particularly where progress in spiritual life was concerned. We were meant to put in common, not just our material goods, but our spiritual possessions too; such as our personal experiences. We were to offer others, in a spirit of humility, whatever seemed a fruit of our "new self."

Since many of us felt called to live this way at practically the same time, we began to practice it together; and it was not long, before we had understood and were putting into practice the new commandment of Jesus: "Love one another as I have loved you" (Jn. 15:12).

It became more and more evident that God was urging us to seek his reign, not only within us, but among us. His kingdom would grow in each of us as a result of our trying to have it present among us. That meant making our journey to God, not alone, but together; desiring to become holy, not individually, but in company with others, many others.

In our desire for holiness—which in itself is something beautiful and wonderful—we Christians have often been somewhat spiritually self-centered. So we were grateful to God, that he had opened up a way that was new to us: the *way of love*. And love is the *bond of perfection*.

It was a way that could only be followed together.

Although electricity has the potential to produce light, light is actually produced in an electric bulb only when the two poles make contact, and current flows between them. In a similar way, when mutual love was flowing between us, uniting our hearts, it caused us to experience something new: we felt we were experiencing the meaning of the words, "Where two or three are gathered in my name, there am I in their midst" (Mt. 18:20).

Jesus, the most perfect example of a brother, was spiritually present in our midst. And he alone gave meaning to our new way of life, in which we were all brothers and sisters. Otherwise, it would hardly have been worthwhile to leave father, mother, brothers, sisters, and a natural family which had God's blessing, if we were not then going to be part of a supernatural family with Jesus among us.

It was his presence in our midst that led us to understand what he meant in his Priestly Prayer, "That all may be one" (Jn. 17:21). And we feel, that the unity for which he prayed before he died, can be fully realized only by Jesus present in the midst of those united in his name.

Jesus in our midst! What an extraordinary experience!

Perhaps we can never state with absolute certainty that he is in our midst in this or that moment, since his presence presupposes that we are in the state of grace, and one cannot be absolutely certain of being in the grace of God.

But this much *is* certain: when our life together was based on the sincere intention of being ready to die for one another as Jesus asks of us, and when this intention was reflected consistently in our actions—in line with the admonition, "Above all, let your love for one another be constant" (1 Pt. 4:8)—we very often felt that we could sense his presence.

It was like this: just as one feels joy and sorrow, anxiety and doubt, similarly—but at a deeper spiritual level—we experienced that the spiritual presence of Jesus among us gave us an inner peace that was his alone; fullness of joy that only he could give; and a strength and conviction that were not so much the fruit of reason or will, but a special gift from God.

His presence was always a more-than-abundant recompense for every sacrifice we might have made; and it more than justified every step we had taken for him and toward him in this new way of life. It helped us to see situations and things in their true light. It gave us comfort in times of sorrow, and equilibrium when we were elated.

Each of us who trusted in Jesus' words with child-like wonder, and put them into practice without hairsplitting and rationalizations, enjoyed that fore-taste of heaven, which is the kingdom of God in the midst of those united in his name.

Jesus in our midst! That is what the Focolare is all about.

But it was on occasions when his presence in our midst diminished through some fault of our own, that we understood best how much his presence meant.

At such times we did not feel at all tempted to go back to the world we had left. The experience of having Jesus in our midst had been far too powerful for us to be attracted by the petty vanities of the world, which his divine presence had put in proper perspective.

It was more like a shipwreck, where people grab

for anything they can get their hands on to save themselves. We grasped about for any method the Gospel might suggest to restore our fragmented unity.

However, simply making an act of the will on those occasions when we felt his presence among us had diminished, was not enough. Rather, just as two crossed logs feed the flames as they themselves are consumed, we saw, that if we wanted to have Jesus constantly present among us, we had to live, moment by moment, all those virtues—such as patience, prudence, gentleness, poverty, purity, and so on— which are necessary to maintain supernatural unity with our brothers and sisters. We could not simply procure Jesus' presence among us once and for all, because Jesus is alive, his presence is dynamic.

"Where two or three..." We frequently had occasion to marvel at the practical implications of these mysterious and divine words.

"Where two or three..." Jesus does not specify who. He leaves it anonymous: "Where two or three," whoever they may be. They could be two or three repentant sinners united in his name, two or three young women like we were, a little child and an adult—as long as there were two or three.

Putting these words into practice, we have seen barriers crumble on every side. One such barrier has been the narrow-minded, fault-finding, and even hateful attitude often existing between persons of different neighborhoods, towns, or regions. Jesus among us overcame these examples of foolish human weakness then, for example, someone from Trent and someone from Rovereto (a neighboring town) were united in his name.

Where there were two or more from different countries, the barrier of nationalism crumbled.

Where there were two or more from different racial backgrounds, racism crumbled.

Two or more—whoever they were, when they had always been considered incompatible for reasons of culture, class, age, or whatever. All could be, and indeed were meant to be, united in the name of Christ.

And where two or more good-living, church-going persons were united in his name, the spirit of rivalry that so often reigned among members of different church organizations or religious communities would disappear.

The practice of living according to these words gave our community and our gatherings something of the atmosphere of the early Christian communities, helping to show the world that the Church is everyone's Mother and a shining example of unity.

These words also pointed out the communitarian aspect of the Christian life, taking us beyond the individualistic approach that many Christians had, and which seemed outdated.

A spirituality based on these words was not one

that required a great preparation, or that was just for experts in the spiritual life. It seemed an ideal of life suitable for everyone. After all, Jesus had not said, "Where two or three *saints* are gathered in my name, there am I," but, "Where two or three...."

To understand what it really means to have Jesus in our midst, we have to experience it. But we can attempt to explain it by comparing it to the Gospel story of the disciples of Emmaus (Lk. 24:13-35).

Some years ago, a group of us visited the Holy Land, and it was truly a unique experience. Several of the holy places made a very deep impression on us, and we felt touched by God's grace. One of these places was Emmaus. We went there one sunny afternoon, and a golden sunset awaited us. When we reached our destination, got out of the car, and walked the same street that Jesus might have walked, we recalled all that had happened there so many years before.

It had taken place on the third day after Jesus' death, the day he rose from the dead. Two of his disciples had set out from Jerusalem, bound for the little town of Emmaus about seven miles away. While they were conversing, a man approached and began to walk along with them. He asked: "What are you discussing?" They answered: "Are you the only one in Jerusalem who doesn't know what has happened there these last few days, how Jesus of Nazareth, a prophet who was powerful in word and deed, was crucified?" Jesus replied: "How foolish you are, and slow to believe! Didn't the Messiah have to suffer all this?" And he went on to explain the Scriptures to them.

When they arrived at Emmaus and the disciples saw that he intended to go further, they said: "Stay with us, since it is getting late." Jesus went in with them, and at the breaking of the bread they recognized him. Then he disappeared. And they remarked to one another: "Were not our hearts burning within us while he was with us?"

Perhaps nothing explains as well as these words, the experience we had from the very beginning of the Focolare—the experience of living with Jesus in our midst. For when Jesus is present—even if it is "only" spiritually—he is still Jesus; he explains the Scriptures to us, and our hearts burn with his love, which is Life. Once we have experienced his presence, we never want to be without it; and so we too say: "Stay with us, Lord, because it is getting late. Without you it is darkest night."

Throughout these years, Jesus' presence in the Focolare has had enormous consequences. First and foremost, countless people have found God or returned to him, which, as I said before, is the principal effect of the Focolare's life. And the Focolare has now spread everywhere.

Jesus in our midst has touched people's hearts, and changed them as he alone can. He has borne witness to himself. Thus, all who have materially or spiritually left everything to obtain his presence—that "precious pearl" of the Gospel—have seen the world around them change.

When people encounter Jesus present in a community—be it large or small—few are able to resist him. He, who is the Light of the world, enlightens them. He, who is the Fire of Love, warms their hearts. As a consequence, persons who perhaps did not believe in him before, now believe; because, in a way, they have spiritually seen him.

Thus, even atheists, public sinners and prostitutes—among others—have been converted to Christ and become his followers,

In this encounter with Jesus present among those united in his name, persons who were lukewarm or vacillating in their faith, and priests beset by trials, have found new fervor and peace, and a new appreciation for the life they have chosen. And they have become more resolute in doing God's will.

However, just as Jesus—when he lived on earth—was not concerned exclusively with saving people's souls, so too, Jesus in our midst has shown us a way to meet many of our material needs.

Living in the light of his presence, we have come to a deeper understanding of his words, "If two of you join your voices on earth to pray for anything whatever, it shall be granted you by my Father in heaven" (Mt. 18:19). We have acted on these words in many, many situations, and experienced how true they are.

Every time we had to pray for some spiritual or material need, we would pray together; and thus we received countless favors of all kinds, a clear sign to us of God's intervention.

This has become the way of praying *par excellence* in the Focolare.

We must also point out a third effect of Jesus' presence among us. From the beginning, we felt that our new understanding of the Gospel, and of Scripture in general, was a fruit of his presence. Similarly, we soon began to realize that he in our midst was leading us to a deeper understanding of what the pope and the bishops had to say. It was as if their teachings found an echo in our hearts.

Moreover, the dogmas of our faith—that we had sometimes heard criticized by intellectuals with little or no faith—now began to seem more obviously true. It was no longer just a matter of having to accept them blindly; they now seemed less obscure to us. While remaining mysteries, they were nonetheless more comprehensible.

This sense of the Church, of the hierarchy, and of the Church's teaching, convinced us from within, that a life with Jesus in our midst could make people real champions of the Church, who would be able to defend her against error; not so much because they had studied theology (which would, of course, be very useful), but especially because they had this interior understanding of the Church, this sense of being one with the Church.

It also seemed to us that a spirituality based on Jesus in our midst could prepare people for one of the most important tasks of our day: the dialogue with the world.

This innate sense for the truth enables us to reach out to those who are in error, and to appreciate whatever elements of truth they may already have found.

If we were asked what else the presence of Jesus in our midst means to the Focolare, we would have to answer that he has been its *founder* and its *legislator*, in the sense that the Focolare now has a certain structure which has been approved by the Church; and this structure is simply the result of our efforts, day by day, to discern the various ideas that we felt Jesus was suggesting to us, as we tried to live in unity with one another and with the hierarchy.

Moreover, Jesus in our midst has been the best *propagator* of the Focolare, through the witness of unity: "That they may be one in us, that the world may believe" (Jn. 17:21).

He is the *sustainer* of the Focolare. His presence, even in the most painful and difficult moments, has practically always been our one comfort; both at the headquarters of the Focolare and in every part of the world where it exists.

If the Focolare has such powerful effects, it is because of him. And if it has been officially recognized by the Church, we think it is because one and the same Christ is present in the Focolare and in the hierarchy.

Jesus in our midst is our *Commander-in-Chief* in the battles which the Focolare is called to wage on all fronts: those where the lines have been established and need to be held and fortified; and other positions, at first unknown to us, where Jesus sends us from time to time. For God alone knows his complete plan for the Focolare, and Jesus in our midst reveals it to us a little at a time.

Jesus in our midst is also the real *superior* of every Focolare household. Because of the love that circulates among the members, he enlightens those charged with guiding others. But he also does this, because those in positions of responsibility have a special grace to teach others, first and foremost, that their top priority must always be to have Jesus present in their midst.

When a Focolare household, or a center, or a branch, or region of the Focolare is set up according to the guidelines that God has given us and the Church has approved, then in some way God speaks through those in authority. For in this Movement, that he has raised up, nourished, molded and structured, those in authority have but one task: to interpret his wishes.

When Jesus is in our midst, it seems that Divine Wisdom gives order to everything in a very dynamic way. All share in this Wisdom and take delight in it, and feel that they are exactly where they belong; just where God wants them to be.

From the newest Focolare household, to the families that live this spirituality; from two or three congressmen united in Jesus' name, to a group of Benedictines living this spirit; from those who live this way in Africa, to those in America—wherever there is a nucleus of the Focolare, there the light of Jesus in our midst shines brightly.

The fact that Jesus in our midst is the fruit of our mutual love, makes us a bit like Mary: we too, in a spiritual way, are God's instruments for giving Jesus to the world. This is why, in the Catholic Church, the Focolare is also known as the Work of Mary.

At the beginning of the Focolare, we left everything, to choose God alone.

When we live the spirituality he has given us, and put his will into practice, it seems that the exalted and unique Ideal that we chose amidst the ruins of the war has come down from heaven to dwell among us: Jesus in our midst.

Notes

[1] Galatians 5:22.

[2] In the Catholic Church, the word spirituality is used to indicate a specific way in which people try to accomplish the ideal of the Christian life. The author refers to the Focolare spirituality, which emphasizes unity.

[3] Patriarch Athenagoras and Chiara Lubich had many other fruitful encounters in the years following this initial visit. Important dialogue with the Orthodox Church continued with his successor Demetrios I and still continues today with Bartholomeos I. In 1977, Chiara Lubich's reception of the Templeton Prize for progress in religion gave the impetus for the Focolare's involvement in the dialogue with the world's great religions. Promising exchange has begun with Jews, Moslems, Hindus, Buddhists and others. A dialogue also exists today with people who have no particular belief in God. Some of them, after having come into contact with the life proposed by the Focolare, have found faith. Others grasp this message of unity that goes beyond every barrier, and collaborate to promote peace, unity, and a civilization of love. For more information on these dialogues, see *Unity–Our Adventure* (New York: New City Press, 1987), pp. 57-61, and *Chiara Lubich–A Life For Unity* (London/ New York/Manila: New City, 1992), pp. 118-25.

[4] "Leggenda dei tre compagni" in *Fonti Francescane*, I (Assisi, 1977), p. 1082.

[5] See Matthew 7:21, John 14:21.

[6] St. Francis de Sales, *Treatise on the Love of God*, VIII, 7.

[7] "Let me hear what God the Lord will speak, for he will speak peace to his people, to his saints, to those who turn to him in their hearts" (Psalm 85:8 RSV).

[8] Ephesians 4:22; Romans 6:6; Colossians 3:9.

[9] "Over all these virtues put on love, which binds the rest together and makes them perfect" (Colossians 3:14).

[10] St. Augustine, Sermon 271, PL 38-39, 1245.

[11] Over 100 summer Mariapolises now take place each year throughout the world. There are permanent Mariapolises in Europe, Africa, Asia, North and South America and Australia.

[12] This work, traditionally attributed to St. Bonaventure, is now thought to be the work of Giacomo da Milano. Its doctrinal content, however, is clearly Bonaventure's, and is drawn from his mystical works (cf. *Mystical Vine*, ch. 24).

[13] Letter 70 in *Epistolario*, III (Alba, 1966), p. 109.

[14] Letters 333, 102, 159 in *Epistolario*, III (Alba, 1966), p. 91, 23, 162.

[15] See *Thérèse of Lisieux–A Discovery of Love* (New York: New City Press, 1992), p. 98.